Need to Know
Teenage Sex

Caroline Carter

Heinemann
LIBRARY

www.heinemann.co.uk/library
Visit our website to find out more information about **Heinemann Library** books.

To order:

 Phone 44 (0) 1865 888066

 Send a fax to 44 (0) 1865 314091

 Visit the Heinemann Bookshop at www.heinemann.co.uk/library to browse our catalogue and order online.

Produced by Roger Coote Publishing
Gissing's Farm, Fressingfield, Suffolk IP21 5SH, UK

First published in Great Britain by Heinemann Library, Halley Court, Jordan Hill, Oxford OX2 8EJ, part of Harcourt Education.
Heinemann is a registered trademark of Harcourt Education Ltd.

Editorial: Katie Orchard
Design: Jane Hawkins
Picture Research: Lynda Lines
Consultant: Christina Thompson
Production: Viv Hichens

Originated by Ambassador Litho Ltd
Printed and bound in China by South China Printing Company

ISBN 0 431 09821 2
07 06 05 04 03
10 9 8 7 6 5 4 3 2 1

British Library Cataloguing in Publication Data
Carter, Caroline
Teenage sex. - (Need to know)
1.Teenagers - Sexual behaviour - Juvenile literature 2.Sex instruction for teenagers - Juvenile literature
I.Title
306.7'0835

Acknowledgements
The publishers would like to thank the following for permission to reproduce photographs:
Corbis p. 5 (Jonathan Cavendish); Corbis Stock Market pp. 10 (Nancy Ney), 27 (Jim Erickson); Hodder Wayland Picture Library pp. 7 (Angela Hampton), 15, 17, 22 (Tizzie Knowles), 44; Hulton Archive p. 8; Medipics pp. 24–25 (Malcolm Earl), 26, 31 (Dan McCoy/Rainbow); Network Photographers *front cover* (Justin Leighton); Photofusion pp. 6 (Ute Klaphake), 46 (Paul Baldesare); Popperfoto pp. 11 (Reuters), 19 (Dave Joyner/PPP Athletics); Rex Features pp. 1 (John Mantel), 14 (Paul Brown), 18 (Sipa), 20 (Amanda Knapp), 28, 30 (Phanie/Alix), 36 (John Mantel), 38, 43 (Nick Cobbing), 45 (John Powell); Science Photo Library pp. 29 (Juergen Berger, Max Planck Institute), 33 (Tek Image), 48 (Jim Varney); Still Pictures p. 51 (Mark Edwards); Topham Picturepoint pp. 12 (Image Works), 34 (Image Works), 39 (Image Works), 40 (Bob Daemmrich/Image Works). Artwork by Alex Pang and Michael Posen.

Every effort has been made to contact copyright holders of any material reproduced in this book. Any omissions will be rectified in subsequent printings if notice is given to the publishers.

Any words appearing in the text in bold, **like this**, are explained in the Glossary.

Contents

Teenage sex

Fifty years ago teenage sex was a taboo subject. It was hardly discussed at all, except when a young girl was unlucky enough to get pregnant before she was married. It must have seemed that hardly anyone had sex until they were in their twenties.

The widespread silence and shame surrounding teenage sex allowed ignorance to flourish. There was no such thing as 'sex education', and people could not talk about sex, so they lacked information. Instead, teenagers had to base their actions on playground gossip, rumours and myths. Teenage boys were often told that **masturbation** was sinful and harmful. Teenage girls were told almost nothing at all – about masturbation or sex.

Today it is almost impossible to open a magazine, read a problem page, go to see a film, visit a teen website, even watch *The Simpsons*, without hearing about teenage sex. In fact, it can sometimes seem as though everyone is having sex – all the time.

Is everyone 'doing it'?

The message coming from the media, loud and clear, is that not only is everyone 'doing it', but they all find having sex as easy as eating an ice cream. There is rarely any anxiety about sex on screen. In most TV dramas, for instance, whether the couples appear passionate or tender, excited or bored with each other, they never seem to have any problems actually having sex. Sex itself is never shown to be disappointing. It is the 'relationship' that comes with problems attached.

The media portrayal of sex as a kind of 'no-worries' Disneyland for adults is a powerful if silent pressure on modern teenagers. Today's teenagers face all kinds of anxieties about being 'good at sex' and measuring up to the adult world – anxieties that many parents did not have when they were young.

There may even have been some advantages to the forbidden, secret nature of sex in the past for teenagers – there was no one saying: 'to be an adult, you must become sexually active as soon as possible and enjoy it every time'. Instead, the message was more like: 'sex is dangerous and full of suffering, but sweet'.

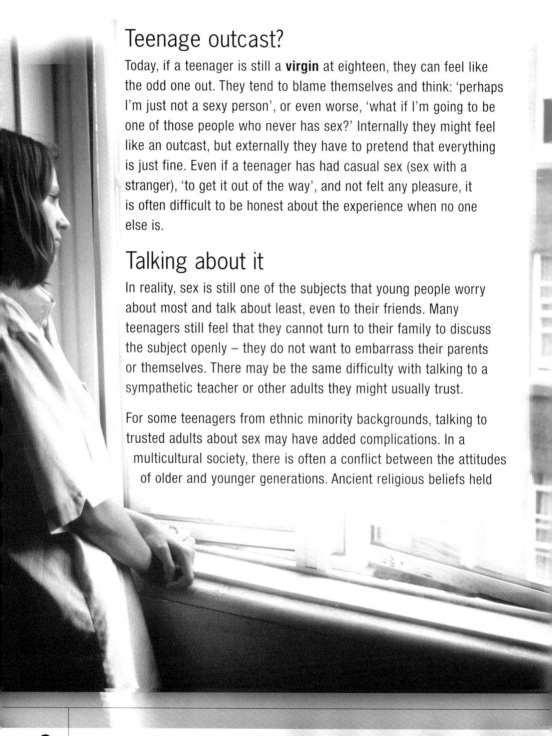

Teenage outcast?

Today, if a teenager is still a **virgin** at eighteen, they can feel like the odd one out. They tend to blame themselves and think: 'perhaps I'm just not a sexy person', or even worse, 'what if I'm going to be one of those people who never has sex?' Internally they might feel like an outcast, but externally they have to pretend that everything is just fine. Even if a teenager has had casual sex (sex with a stranger), 'to get it out of the way', and not felt any pleasure, it is often difficult to be honest about the experience when no one else is.

Talking about it

In reality, sex is still one of the subjects that young people worry about most and talk about least, even to their friends. Many teenagers still feel that they cannot turn to their family to discuss the subject openly – they do not want to embarrass their parents or themselves. There may be the same difficulty with talking to a sympathetic teacher or other adults they might usually trust.

For some teenagers from ethnic minority backgrounds, talking to trusted adults about sex may have added complications. In a multicultural society, there is often a conflict between the attitudes of older and younger generations. Ancient religious beliefs held by immigrant parents can often clash with the 21st-century Western ideas embraced by their children.

There is not just one typical experience of sex for teenagers – and there never has been. There have been **gay** teenagers, for example, for thousands of years, although they have struggled against social prejudice and repression since at least early medieval times. Famously, the ancient Greeks elevated the love between an older man and a younger boy above the love in a **heterosexual** relationship.

No one is alone

The new media openness about sex means that there are now many organizations with websites and phone helplines, which can provide information and advice on many aspects of the subject, in confidence. (For a list of useful contacts see pages 52–53.) Whatever anxieties a person might have, there is no longer any need to suffer in silence.

Sometimes it helps to talk through worries or anxieties in confidence with a trusted adult.

History of teenage sex

In Victorian times girls often married young, and teenage brides were a common sight.

The history of sexual freedom for anyone in the West, let alone teenagers, is very short – going back only as far as the 1960s. Teenage sex, on the other hand, has been around for a long time – girls were often married before the age of 20. Young adults in their teens often had families of their own to support. The word 'teenager', meaning someone between childhood and adulthood, was not used until the 1950s. A post-war economic boom created a new generation with very different ideas and aspirations from their parents. And for the first time in history, many young people were not going out to work at the age of fourteen, but studying and still living with their parents.

This relative freedom was unthinkable 400 years ago, when harsh economic necessity ruled people's lives. Boys were apprenticed to their employers and lived away from home from an early age. Unmarried teenage girls were treated as the property of their fathers – their **virginity** was valued as their only asset.

Sex outside marriage was unlawful whether it was by rape or by consent. It is said that clerks of the Elizabethan court used shorthand for the name of the offence ('For Unlawful Carnal Knowledge'), accidentally creating the most infamous four-letter word in the English language.

Teenage prostitutes were common in 19th-century London, driven into the trade by starvation wages. Only young people whose parents kept them in food and shelter could afford to remain virtuous and free of infection. **Syphilis** had ravaged Europe since the 1500s. It was treated with mercury, which could kill the patient quicker than the disease.

It was not until after the Second World War that attitudes towards sexuality began to change in some parts of the Western world. In 1968, the **contraceptive** pill became available on prescription for married women over 21 in Australia and in the UK. By 1967, in England, Scotland and Wales, **abortion** had been legalized under strict criteria. In the same year, **homosexual** sex between two consenting adults was decriminalized (no longer treated as a criminal act), although not for teenage **gays**. The **age of consent** for male gays was 21 until it was reduced to 18 in 1994 and to 16 in 2000.

Sex and society

Today it is easy to forget that it was only 60 years ago that 'nice girls' (meaning marriageable girls) were not expected to want sex and were certainly not expected to enjoy it. Instead they were meant to lose their **virginity** to their husbands and treat sex as one of their duties as wives. This created a double standard, since men were not expected to be virgins when they married.

By the 1970s, young people's ideas about marriage and sexuality were changing. As the restrictions on prescribing the **contraceptive** pill were lifted, more and more young women gained control over their own fertility. Women found themselves free to have several sexual relationships before committing to one person and raising a family. Couples no longer automatically decided to get married.

Limits to freedom

Today, health concerns have brought an end to some of the sexual freedoms of the 1960s and 1970s. The threat of infection by the sexually transmitted **HIV** virus has sent shock waves through society since the 1980s. Wearing **condoms** to prevent sexual infection of any kind, as well as preventing pregnancy, is the safest course of action.

In some countries around the world, religious law still defines the nature of all sexual relationships. For example, in the Republic of Ireland, divorce is not permitted and **abortion** is still illegal. Many Muslim countries also have laws about certain sexual relationships. Under Islamic law **heterosexual** sex is only lawful in marriage. **Homosexuality** is illegal.

During Taliban rule in Afghanistan, these teenage girls had to cover their hair and their faces by law.

Age of consent

From ancient times, the law has given special protection to minors (those considered too young to understand the consequences of their actions). The '**age of consent**' defines the legal age at which a person may consent to sexual activity, including **sexual intercourse** with another person. Sexual intercourse means penetration of the **vagina** or anus by a penis. To have legal sex, both people have to be at the age of consent or older. The age of consent can vary from country to country, and from state to state in the USA (see table on page 49).

Puberty and beyond

Most young people become interested in sex at puberty – a time of great physical change and, often, emotional turmoil. Mood swings and irritability are natural side effects of the many changes the body goes through. In her autobiography, Victoria Beckham, the showbiz celebrity, remembers being a lonely teenager. She was always being teased about her acne and was nicknamed 'Sticky Vicky'.

Becoming a woman

Girls can start developing sexually as young as ten and as old as thirteen – there is no right age. Pubic hair around the genitals appears first, followed by underarm hair. Breasts start to develop: they may be soft or firm, droop downwards or point up. Nipples may be large or small, pale or dark. All these differences are normal.

Most girls start menstruating between the ages of ten and sixteen, although some start earlier. This means that a girl is able to become pregnant. A tiny, **unfertilized egg** is shed from her body every month, together with the womb lining. Menstrual bleeding (a period) usually lasts about four days. Period pains may start about a year after periods begin. They are due to large contractions of the womb muscle. A hot water bottle and a painkiller normally help. The **contraceptive** pill may relieve symptoms of severe period pain, but should only be taken under medical supervision.

Female sexual organs

The **vulva** is the area around the opening to the **vagina** including the labia (lips) and the **clitoris**, beneath the mons pubis (pubic mound covered with hair). The vagina is a hollow, muscular tube, which reaches up inside to the **cervix**, the closed opening to the womb. The vagina expands and contracts, allowing it to accommodate something as slim as a tampon and as wide as a baby. The vaginal opening may be covered by a thin piece of tissue called the hymen, which historically was thought to prove a girl's **virginity**.

The inner lips (labia minora) are thinner than the outer lips (labia majora) and join at the front to form the clitoris – source of the female **orgasm**. The outer lips form a hood over the clitoris at the top and extend back to just in front of the anus.

Girls feel sexual excitement, just like boys, but for girls the feelings and sensations are internal. Girls may notice a slight milky discharge from the vagina when they become sexually excited.

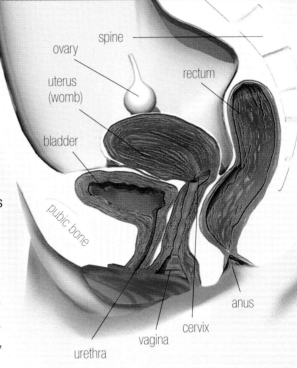

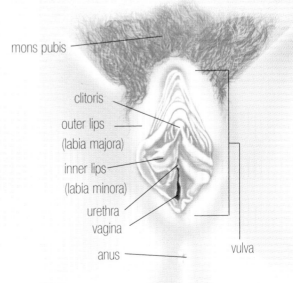

13

Becoming a man

For boys, sexual development can happen at any time between the ages of ten and eighteen, but usually begins around thirteen or fourteen. Development often carries on into the late teens and early twenties.

A dramatic increase in levels of the male hormone testosterone triggers the body changes that boys begin to experience from about the age of eleven. Around this time, boys begin to develop deeper voices. This process usually happens gradually, but the voice can 'break' overnight. Some boys start to grow facial hair and need to shave regularly. Hair can also grow on the chest, legs, arms and genital area. Many teenage boys experience acne. Their arms and legs begin to grow longer, stronger and more muscular. Boys' shoulders widen and their genitals grow bigger.

By the time most teenage boys are fourteen, their testosterone levels will have increased by almost 800 per cent. They will experience waves of strong sexual feelings, which cause **erections**. When an erection occurs, special tube-like passageways inside the penis fill up with blood, making the penis hard and straight, and forcing it to stand away from the body. Males of all ages have erections, including babies and old men. Boys do not **ejaculate** until they have reached sexual maturity, at around the age of twelve or older.

During puberty, a boy's penis seems to have a life of its own, having erections unexpectedly and ejaculating during sleep after a 'wet dream'.

Personal hygiene becomes especially important, as testosterone affects sweat glands.

This can sometimes be embarrassing, as the ejaculate leaves a milky stain. It is worth remembering that every erection goes down in the end, whether or not a boy ejaculates, or 'comes'. It is said that the easiest way to make an erection go down is to think very hard about something else.

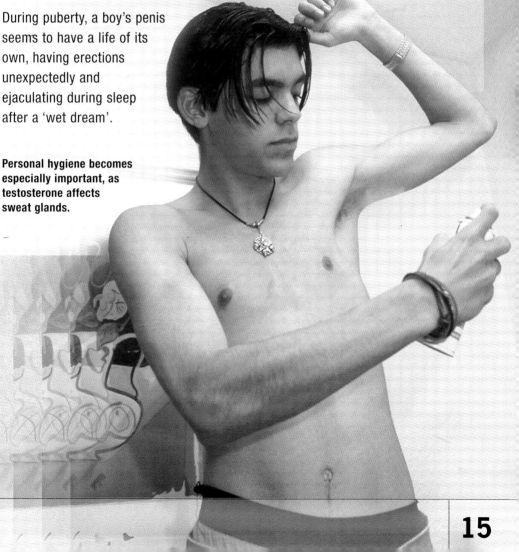

Male sexual organs

The penis has two main parts, a head (glans) and a shaft. The head of the penis is much more sensitive than the shaft. The **foreskin** is a sleeve of skin that surrounds the head of the penis. The foreskin stretches when the penis is **erect** and the head of the penis is completely exposed. This can be painful if the foreskin is tight but it can be eased back gently and gradually, in the bath if necessary. If the foreskin is not washed underneath, everyday, a yellowish-white substance called smegma builds up.

Many men in the world today are circumcised, usually because they were born into the Jewish or Muslim religion. This means that their foreskins were removed during childhood. Circumcision makes no difference to a man's ability to give or receive sexual pleasure.

The **scrotum** is a loose pouch of skin that hangs outside the body, behind the penis, and holds the **testicles**. There are two testicles in the scrotum, which produce tadpole-shaped sperm that join with the female egg to make a baby. Sperm are damaged or killed by heat. The testicles keep the sperm cooler than the internal body temperature of 37°C. **Semen** travels from the testicles to the penis by a series of tubes called the vas deferens and the urethra. The urethra is also attached to the bladder. It is not easy to urinate when the penis is erect because a muscle closes off the bladder.

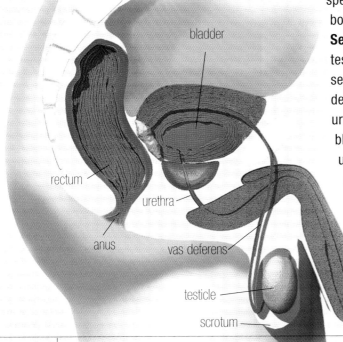

bladder

rectum

urethra

anus

vas deferens

testicle

scrotum

shaft

glans

foreskin

penis

Does size matter?

The ability to have enjoyable **sexual intercourse** is not determined by penis size. Many young men worry that their penis might be smaller than everyone else's. As a rule, the larger a penis is when soft, the less it grows when hard, and vice versa. Most twelve-year-olds, before sexual development, have a penis that is 3–5 cm long when soft, and usually less than 8 cm long when hard.

Adult penis size is usually 6–10 cm long when soft, and about 12–19 cm long when hard. The thickness of a man's erect penis is usually about 3–4 cm across.

Sex without intercourse

Kissing and fondling

Repressed Brits used to think that kissing in public was false and affected. But now, the old touch barriers have broken down, perhaps because the older generation of today were young in the 1960s. In the decade of swinging London, it became normal to see teenagers kissing and fondling each other in public.

Masturbation

Masturbation involves sexually stimulating the body to **orgasm** by hand, without engaging in the act of **sexual intercourse**. Most boys rub the shaft of their penis by hand to get an **erection** and to have an orgasm. Girls may not talk so much about masturbation but many of them do it, by stimulating the area around the **clitoris**. It is normal and natural for teenagers to explore their own sexual responses using their own bodies, in private.

❝The world is divided into three categories of men: those who know where your clitoris is, those who don't, and those who are still looking.❞

Cadillac Carter, *Hidden Treasure – The Pleasure Organ*

Both sexes have fantasies while they masturbate. It is a way to relax and let go of inhibitions. Anxieties dissolve and it is easier to reach orgasm. Some people feel guilty about this, perhaps because the practice has been condemned for so long. But unlike sexual intercourse, self-masturbation is completely harmless, and will not lead to pregnancy or infection.

Oral sex

Couples can sexually stimulate each other to orgasm without having sexual intercourse, through **oral sex**. This kind of mutual masturbation means using the mouth and tongue to stimulate each other's genitals, known as giving a 'blow job' to a boy and 'giving head' to a girl. Oral sex is a very intimate act and no one should feel forced to participate in it. There can also be health risks (see pages 28 and 31).

Secret of success?

Energy is not 'lost' through masturbation, although some athletes will not masturbate or have sex the night before a competition because they believe it affects their drive. This superstition may stem from the ancient Greeks' belief that each man had only a limited amount of **semen** and that every time he spilt some, he died a little.

Contrary to popular myth, abstaining from sex does not improve a person's athletic prowess.

The act of sex

Sex is one of the most intimate acts that a couple can share – a hurried or awkward experience can be unpleasant. Most people like to find a private, secure and comfortable place for sex, such as a bed. Parents usually draw the line at allowing their teenage children to have sex at home and anyway, trying to have sex in earshot of the family TV is very inhibiting. Upstairs at a party a couple is also likely to be interrupted. Even if a teenage couple have been able to find a place where they will not be disturbed, they may still feel awkward and clumsy with each other, especially if they are both **virgins** and unsure what to expect.

Foreplay

Usually a couple who are planning to have sex build up to it first. It helps relax both people involved. They can talk together about how they are feeling and find out what gives their partner pleasure. They stroke each other's bodies, kiss and hold each other very close. This build-up is called foreplay.

As the man becomes excited, or aroused, his penis grows and becomes hard and **erect**. If they are using a male **condom**, he usually rolls one over his penis now. When the woman is aroused, her **vagina** becomes moist. The lips of her **vulva** and her **clitoris** become swollen and they feel more sensitive.

Intercourse

When she feels she is ready, the woman may guide the tip of the man's penis to the opening of her vagina. The man then gently thrusts the whole of his penis upwards to fill the vagina and pulls it back again. The man and woman move together rhythmically in this way, gradually becoming more stimulated.

Orgasm

If a woman's clitoris becomes highly sensitized, the muscles in her vagina will react with spasms of pleasure and she will reach **orgasm**. When a man reaches orgasm, the muscles at the base of his penis contract hard and **semen** spurts out of the tip. During a man's orgasm, about 3–15 contractions occur. The first three or so are usually the most intense.

Shere Hite reported in a survey of American women in 1976 that it was rare for women to reach orgasm during **sexual intercourse** because they needed more clitoral stimulation just before sex. It is useful to understand this to help make sex equally enjoyable for both people.

Preventing pregnancy

People use various methods to prevent pregnancy, some of which are more effective than others. The most effective way of preventing an unwanted pregnancy and any sexually transmitted infection (**STI**) is by practising **abstinence** – saying no to **sexual intercourse** – until marriage or both partners feel they are in a steady relationship.

The most unreliable method of all is to rely on the boy withdrawing his penis from the **vagina** before he **ejaculates**. There are sperm in the fluid at the end of the penis – and it only takes one sperm to cause pregnancy.

The 'rhythm' method

Some religions teach that the only purpose of sexual intercourse is to have children, so using **contraceptives** must be against religious law. Orthodox Roman Catholics are forbidden to use the contraceptive pill for this reason and many use the **rhythm method** instead. This involves avoiding sexual intercourse around the time of **ovulation**, when a woman is most likely to become pregnant.

This method is not very effective as sperm can survive in the vagina for up to five days and it only takes one sperm out of the average 300 million in the ejaculate to fertilize an egg. For the same reason, having sex during a girl's period will not necessarily prevent pregnancy.

In a loving relationship, a couple usually shares responsibility for preventing pregnancy.

There is a device called Persona, which is a test-based version of the rhythm method. The device is available over the counter but it is expensive to buy and requires following a strict regime of urine tests for ten days every month. The monitor must be personally customized for two months before it can be used. It offers no protection against **HIV** or STIs but it has no side effects. The UK Department of Health has cast doubt on its efficiency because certain medications can affect its accuracy. It is advisable to consult a GP before buying this device.

Contraceptives

Contraceptives are devices and pills that prevent pregnancy. Although there are a lot of different methods, some are not ideal for everyone. Non-barrier methods, such as the pill, cannot give protection against STIs or HIV. Contraceptive devices that must be inserted into the uterus, such as the IUD ('coil'), are thought to work by creating a low-level infection in the womb and may represent a health risk for young girls.

Preventing pregnancy

When choosing which **contraceptive** method to use, it is best to get advice from a doctor or family planning expert. Some of those listed on these pages should only be used under medical supervision.

	Method	Reliability	Availability	
Barrier methods	Female **condoms**	95 per cent effective if used correctly	Over the counter	
	Male condoms	94–98 per cent effective if used correctly	Over the counter, from dispensing machines or free from clinics	
	Vaginal diaphragms/ Cervical caps	92–96 per cent effective if used correctly	Free from a GP or clinic	
	Vaginal sponge	90 per cent effective if used correctly	Over the counter	
Hormonal contraception	The combined pill	99 per cent effective	Prescription only	
	The mini pill	Over 98 per cent effective	Prescription only	
	Depo-provera injection	99 per cent effective	Prescription only, given by a doctor	
Emergency contraception	The 'morning-after' pill	95 per cent effective within 24 hours of **unprotected sex***	Over the counter in the UK and free from clinics and GPs	
	Intra-Uterine Device (IUD)	98 per cent effective if fitted within five days of unprotected sex	An IUD must be fitted (and removed) by a trained doctor	

* Consists of two doses of a special pill, which must be taken 72 hours apart, beginning not more than 72 hours after intercourse. The pills delay the release of an egg from an ovary, or change the womb lining slightly for a short time, so a fertilized egg cannot implant. Reliability drops from 95 per cent to 85 per cent if taken within 25–48 hours after unprotected sex.

Advantages	Side effects
Can be fitted inside the **vagina** 8 hours before intercourse. Provides rubber and **spermicide** protection against **STIs.**	None
Gives instant protection. Provides rubber and spermicide protection against STIs.	None
Gives instant protection. Provides rubber and spermicide protection against STIs.	**Cystitis** may be a problem
Gives instant protection. Provides spermicide protection against STIs.	None
Provides some protection against pelvic inflammatory disease, ovarian cancer	Dizziness, nausea, changes in menstruation, mood, weight gain. Must be taken every day. Does not provide protection against STIs.
Some protection against pelvic inflammatory disease	Irregular bleeding, weight gain, tender breasts. No instant protection. Must be taken every day at the same time. Does not provide protection against STIs.
Protection against pregnancy for three years	Irregular bleeding. Does not provide protection against STIs.
Early prevention of pregnancy without consequences of later intervention	Possible short-term dizziness, nausea or vomiting
Protection against pregnancy for three to five years	Pelvic infection, if left untreated, can lead to infertility

Background image: Male condoms, available from chemist's, family planning clinics and vending machines.

Becoming pregnant

Unwanted pregnancies happen because **contraception** is not used, or because the chosen method is not properly used or does not work. It may be possible to take emergency contraception in the first five days after **unprotected sex**.

The first sign of pregnancy is usually a missed period. Other signs, which are not always present, are swollen, tender or tingling breasts, darker nipples, nausea or vomiting at any time of day and a frequent need to urinate.

In the UK and Australia, a pregnancy test can be carried out free by a doctor or a family planning clinic, usually on the first day that a period is due. Alternatively, a pregnancy testing kit can be bought over the counter. Kits are expensive but they are just as accurate (99 per cent) as the free tests. Anyone who finds out they are pregnant using a home test kit should still visit their doctor, family planning clinic or

A pregnancy test takes only a few minutes.

pregnancy advisory service. If a teenager decides to have the baby, the visit is important to ensure she receives good healthcare before, during and after giving birth.

An unplanned pregnancy

An unplanned pregnancy can arouse many different feelings. Most women find they have mixed or conflicting feelings. A pregnant teenager may feel worried about being able to cope with a baby, afraid she will have to give up things that are important to her and concerned about how other people may react. At the same time, she might feel happy to learn that she can get pregnant, pleased to have the opportunity to have a baby and excited by a new and unique event in her life.

A pregnant woman has three choices:
- continue the pregnancy and keep the baby
- continue the pregnancy and place the baby for adoption
- end the pregnancy now by having an **abortion**.

Various clinics and organizations offer online counselling and one-to-one appointments for women of all ages who did not plan to be pregnant. The specialist staff at these clinics see many pregnant women who find it difficult to make a decision about what to do.

Sexual health

As well as the possibility of pregnancy, there are serious health risks involved when practising **unprotected sex**. Teenage girls in particular can be putting their bodies at risk when they have sex. Before the age of 20, a girl's **vagina** is more vulnerable to infection because it is still developing. The introduction of **semen** can trigger certain **cervical** conditions. If a teenage girl becomes sexually active, she should go to her doctor for a **smear test** for cervical cancer. This slow-developing cancer can be treated if detected early.

Teenagers may be more at risk of contracting genital **herpes**. Genital and mouth herpes are highly contagious, and can be passed to others through any direct contact when a person has cold sores around the mouth or blisters and sores around the genitals. Personal hygiene is very important to avoid spreading the infection.

Sexually transmitted infections (STIs)

STIs, also known as sexually transmitted diseases, or STDs, are on the increase. This is partly because young people are having unprotected sex with more partners, and partly because they are frightened of telling anyone if they develop an STI. If an STI carrier does not warn sexual partners that they could be infected, there can be very serious consequences. For example, if a young man infected

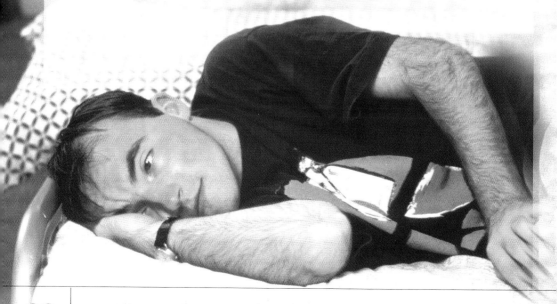

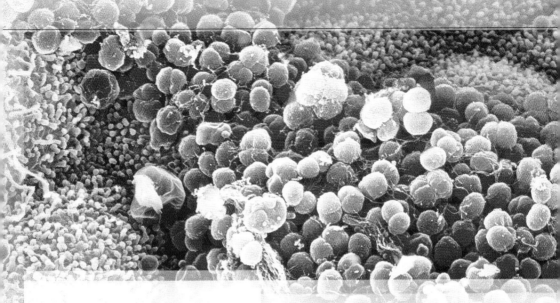

The gonorrhoea microbe as seen under a microscope.

with **chlamydia** does not tell his partner, he may be condemning her to never having children. The symptoms of chlamydia are very mild or absent in women, but if left untreated the infection can cause infertility.

Prevention

Proper use of female or male **condoms** greatly reduces the risk of infection from **gonorrhoea**, **syphilis**, chlamydia, genital warts, **hepatitis B** and **HIV**. **Monogamy** (having sex with only one steady partner) also reduces the risk. **Abstinence** is the only sure-fire protection against all health risks from sex.

Symptoms of STIs

- pain and discomfort when urinating
- any discharge from the penis
- any discharge from the vagina that is unusual (heavier or a different colour, causing soreness, itching or smelling unpleasant)
- pain or itching around the genitals
- lumps, sores, blisters or warts on the genitals.

Treatment

All STIs, except HIV and herpes, can now be cured, usually with antibiotics. Herpes is not curable, but unlike HIV it is not life-threatening and its symptoms can be eased. Anyone who develops any of the symptoms listed above is advised to visit their doctor or a **Genito-urinary medicine (GUM) clinic**. STI carriers should abstain from **sexual intercourse** until they are free from infection. They should inform all their sexual partners, as they may also need treatment.

Sexual health

Human Immunodeficiency Virus (HIV)

HIV attacks the body's immune system, making it difficult, and eventually impossible, to fight off infections. HIV particularly attacks white blood cells. The lower a person's white blood cell count, the weaker their immune system will be.

What is AIDS?

AIDS stands for Acquired Immune Deficiency Syndrome. When a person's immune system has been damaged, he or she is open to other illnesses, especially infections such as tuberculosis and pneumonia, and cancers, many of which would not normally be a threat. Many doctors no longer use the term 'AIDS' to describe this stage. Instead they may refer to this condition as 'late stage' or 'advanced HIV infection'.

How is HIV passed on?

For someone to become infected, a sufficient amount of HIV must get into their blood. The body fluids that contain enough HIV to infect someone are blood, **semen**, **vaginal** fluids including menstrual blood, and breast milk. Saliva, sweat and urine do not contain

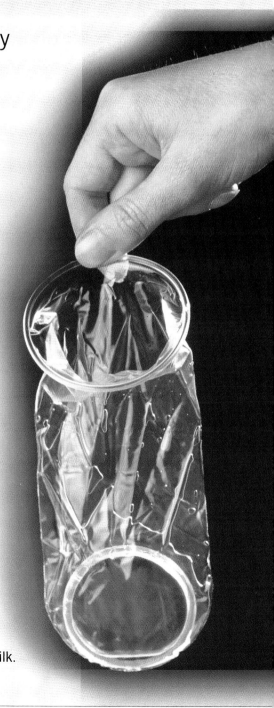

enough of the virus to infect someone. HIV cannot pass through intact external skin, or through the air in the same way as a cold or 'flu virus.

Safer sex

Sexual intercourse using a female or male **condom** is safer sex because HIV cannot pass through the rubber barrier. The male condom should be of high quality, well within its sell-by date, and used correctly, making sure no semen is spilt during withdrawal. Oil-based lubricants and ointments damage condoms and should not be used. (For further information on testing, counselling and treatment for HIV, see page 32.)

Sharing needles could mean passing on HIV-infected blood to another drug-user.

Left: The female condom rarely rips or tears, compared to the male condom, and so is a better method for women to protect themselves from infection.

High risk behaviours for HIV

- Vaginal or **anal sex**, without using a female or male condom (**unprotected sex**).
- There is a small risk of infection through **oral sex** without a condom – HIV can enter the body through sores or cuts in the mouth.
- Sharing hypodermic needles and drug equipment with someone else.

Sexual health

Treatment

The majority of people newly infected with the **HIV** virus are between the ages of 15 and 24 years old. Recent statistics show that the number of young people testing positive for HIV is rising in England and Wales.

If a person has had **unprotected sex** with someone who has HIV (termed HIV positive, or HIV+), or has shared a needle with an intravenous drug-user who is HIV+, they are advised to consider having an HIV test. Once they have been tested, they can receive treatment as soon as possible, if necessary.

Testing for HIV

HIV testing is performed at **GUM clinics** (special clinics where **STIs** are diagnosed and treated in confidence). People who wish to be tested will receive specialized counselling before and after the test. The most commonly used test is an HIV antibody test. The body produces antibodies (blood proteins) in response to the presence of HIV, and this test looks for those antibodies.

The window period

When a person becomes infected with HIV, it can take up to three months for their immune system to produce enough antibodies to show up on an HIV test. (In a few cases it can take up to six months.) This gap is known as the window period.

Since the HIV test looks for antibodies, taking an HIV test less than three months after possibly getting infected might not give an accurate result. However, throughout the window period, the infected person has enough virus in their blood, breast milk or sexual fluids to infect another person, even though the virus will not show up on a test.

Can HIV be treated?

There is no vaccine or cure for HIV. However, anti-HIV drugs are available, and taking a combination of anti-HIV drugs can slow down the damaging effect of HIV on the immune system. There are various helplines offering support, practical help and a listening ear to anyone who is affected by HIV.

This blood test looks for antibodies produced in response to HIV.

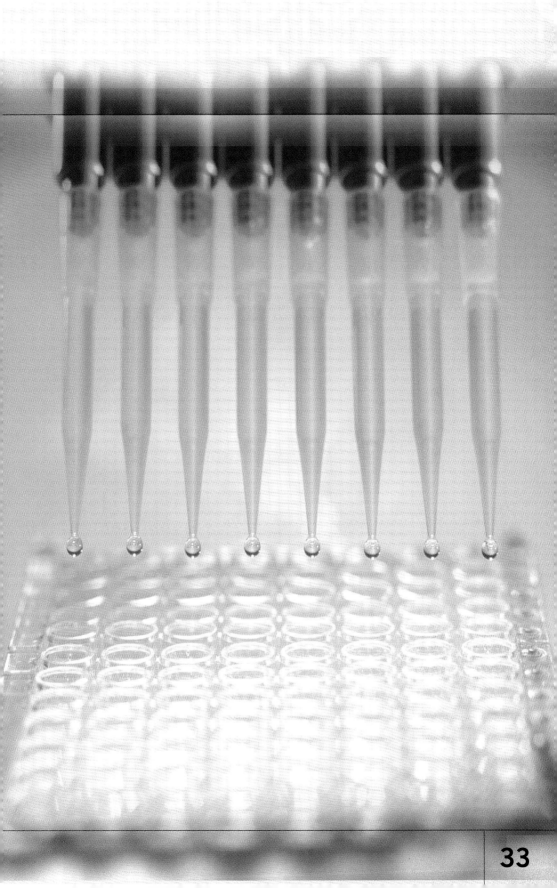

Sex and you

Why don't guys talk?

An important part of sexual intimacy is being able to trust and relate to each other. Lovers need to be able to listen to each other and understand what makes their partner feel comfortable. This may sound obvious but, in the past, it was often more difficult for teenage boys because they were under so much pressure to be tough and manly. Not talking to a partner about what they want from a relationship can lead to uncomfortable misunderstandings.

It is easy to get the wrong idea about what a partner wants when you do not know how to read the signals.

I think Queensland guys are still under a lot of pressure from their fathers to be "Aussie blokes". They've got to play sport, otherwise they're a poofter [gay]. Guys I went to school with, I'd say 99 per cent of them, would say they "couldn't" talk about their emotions. Talking about emotions is for women and any sign of sensitivity is weakness and whingeing ... I tell you, that Aussie-bloke attitude doesn't make you want to sleep with them.

Drew, 21, from Queensland, Australia

Peter's story

Peter, from south-east Australia, describes what happened on one of his 'dates':

'We go for a swim – I want to touch her. I put my arm round her shoulders. She doesn't seem to mind. In fact, I think she likes it. We get back to the beach. We lie down. I roll over and play around a bit, and then I kiss her.

'She says, "Get off!" Quite sharp. I'm blown away. "Look," I say, "you wanted me to kiss you." She starts getting a bit cross. Says she didn't. Just wants to lie here soaking up a bit of sun. "Why did you let me touch you then?" I ask. She says she hugs her friends all the time and her family. It doesn't mean she wants to have sex with them. "Don't you like men?" I ask. She gets really cross then. "Look," she says, "I like sex and men but I also like to feel good about a guy before I sleep with him."

'I thought she'd want to go home, but she calmed down and said she really liked me so she'd explain. She said men and women hardly ever get a chance to get together as friends. I said I knew what she meant. I'm always on edge about having to be some sort of Bruce Springsteen when I'm with girls. She said I've been told lots of things about girls that aren't true. We talked for ages.'

(extract from the Australian website www.secasa.com.au)

Sex and you

When is the right time to start having sex?

Apart from legal age limits (see pages 48–49), there are no schedules for the first time. But however it happens and whether or not it happens in a loving relationship, the first time is rarely as magical as people expect it to be.

Both lovers may be **virgins**, but it does not matter as long as they feel the same way about each other. The problem arises when both partners in a couple have different expectations of sex and they do not talk to each other about how they feel. This can happen easily, to anyone – and not just teenagers.

But for teenagers, the stakes are higher. Older, more experienced people are likely to have more self-confidence and feel more in control. When it is a person's first time and they do not even know the other person, feeling confident is not so easy.

ffWe turned on one another deep drowned gazes, and exchanged a kiss that reduced my bones to rubber and my brain to gruel.**JJ**

Peter De Vries, American novelist 1910–1993

The first time: Andrew's story

'I tried to have sex for the first time when I was fifteen. It was the middle of the afternoon and there was loud traffic outside and bright light. Her mum could have walked in. I was very nervous and so was she. We didn't really know how to do it and I had no idea about foreplay. I just managed to penetrate her once and it was all over! She was understanding about it but I felt terrible. We didn't try again.'

The first time: Kate's story

'I had sex for the first time when I was sixteen with a stranger who was 20 years older than me. It was nothing like I'd expected. Then I had sex with a Frenchman, about 25, who was very experienced but still left me cold. But when I was eighteen I fell in love with a boy in the same year as me at school. Sex with him was wonderful because of our strong relationship. We just came alight when we were together.'

Sex with the wrong person

Everyone makes mistakes. And no one should beat themselves up if they have had sex with someone they regret.

On holiday abroad, drunk or using drugs at a party, sleeping with a good-looking stranger can suddenly seem like a crazy, romantic and spontaneous thing to do. But the morning after, even hours later, the good feelings have often vanished, along with the stranger.

Statistically speaking, only 14 per cent of teenagers' sexual relationships last more than a year, and about as many last only one week. Teenage girls are far more likely to get pregnant after just one sexual encounter because they are more fertile than older women. When a pregnancy results, the relationship almost never endures beyond the crisis (whether the pregnancy continues to term or ends in an **abortion**).

Having casual sex can also have serious health implications. Not knowing the other person means not being able to trust them. Casual sexual partners are far less likely to tell each other if they have a sexually transmitted infection (**STI**), because neither of them expects to see the other again. Having casual sex without a **condom** is self-destructive.

Herpes is very widespread and has no cure. The **contraceptive** pill can make teenage users more susceptible to certain STIs because it alters the **vagina's** acid/alkaline balance. Teenage girls on the pill who have sex with someone infected with **gonorrhoea** increase their chances of catching it from 40 per cent to nearly 100 per cent.

Sex and you

A teenage mother: Becky's story

'I was sixteen and my boyfriend Ben was seventeen. We had been going out together for a few months and we were really close. We started to have **unprotected sex.** We didn't even think twice about the dangers. We didn't think that I would get pregnant. I missed two periods and went to see the doctor. He told me I was pregnant. I didn't know what to do or say. My mum was calm and told me not to worry or get upset.

The relationship of a teenage couple hardly ever survives the crisis of an unplanned pregnancy.

'I went round to Ben's house. When Ben came home, we talked in private. I just said, "I'm pregnant". His reaction shocked me. He put his arms round me and said, "We're having a baby. Becky, I love you!" I was really happy I had a boyfriend who was going to support me and our baby through everything.

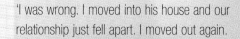

'I was wrong. I moved into his house and our relationship just fell apart. I moved out again.

'Six months went by and I thought I was never going to see Ben again but he turned up on my doorstep, asking me how I was. It felt like before. I thought we were together forever. But he didn't call again.

'I went into labour. I wished that Ben would turn up at the hospital but he didn't. He didn't even know he had a son.

'When Jonathan was a few days old I went looking for Ben. I found him at a friend's house. I showed him Jonathan but he didn't want to know. He didn't even want to hold him.

'Jonathan is one year old now and I'm surviving. It's been very hard and at some points I've felt like giving up but with a lot of help and support from my family and friends, I've been able to get through the dark times. My life hasn't ended like I thought it would. I've managed to finish a college course. And now I can't imagine life without Jonathan. Would I turn back the clock? It's too late for that!'

Extracted from '*Teenage Parenthood*' by the Hangleton & Knoll project in Brighton, UK

Straight, bi or gay?

Being **homosexual** means wanting to have sexual relations with someone who is the same sex as you are. Teenage **gays** have usually been aware of feeling 'different inside' from a young age, perhaps as young as eight or nine. Having gay fantasies or a crush on someone who is of the same sex does not automatically mean that a person is gay. Teenagers can fancy people from the opposite sex (**heterosexual**), the same sex (homosexual), or both sexes (**bisexual**), without necessarily fitting into any of those categories for the rest of their life. It is common for teenagers to feel unsure of their sexuality. Talking to a counsellor, in confidence, can help.

Gay teenagers are often afraid of telling anyone about their feelings because of the prejudice against them that still exists in society. The Equal Opportunities Commission found that 70 per cent of young gays and **lesbians** in Western Australia had suffered gay-hating abuse, and that 25–40 per cent had tried to kill themselves as a result. However, not all gay people suffer such abuse and many come to terms with their sexuality in a supportive, understanding atmosphere.

Teenage and gay: Jake's story

'When I was eleven I found a library book which said that homosexuality was just a phase and I would grow out of it. So that's what I tried to think – that I would end up having a wife and four kids.

'By the time I was fourteen, I was having terrible secret fears. I thought I might be mentally ill or end up in jail. I had no idea that 10 per cent of the urban population was gay and that lots of gays were living happy, fulfilling lives. I thought you had to be like these camp [effeminate] men on TV. And I wasn't.

'I didn't come out to my parents [tell them] until I was 21 and had left home, and I don't regret that. I needed to be sure of myself and have my own support network before I told them.

'I would say to any teenager who thinks they might be gay, remember that you're not alone and there is no need to be frightened.'

It is now much more common for gay men to show their feelings for each other in public.

Sex without consent

Rape means forcing someone to have **sexual intercourse** against their will (without their consent), even if no physical force is used. Rape is an act of violence and is against the law.

If two people are in a relationship and one of them forces the other to have sex, it is still rape. A girl may no longer be a **virgin**, or seem to want sexual intercourse, but if she says 'no', she means no. People know their own limits because they start to feel very uncomfortable once they go over them. Other forms of 'non-consent' include the victim being under the **age of consent**, drunk or drugged, asleep or mentally incapable.

Some facts about rape

Rape has little to do with sexual desire or physical attraction. It is a violent act that is more about anger and aggression and a pathological (abnormal) assertion of power over the victim.

Most rapes take place in the victim's home or the rapist's home. Rapes are most often planned, and in 80 per cent of cases, the rapist knows the victim. Boys are also raped, but the victims are unlikely to report it because of fears of being seen as either **homosexual** or abnormal.

Even if a girl is dressed in a way that some men may find provocative, if she says she does not want to have sex, that is what she means.

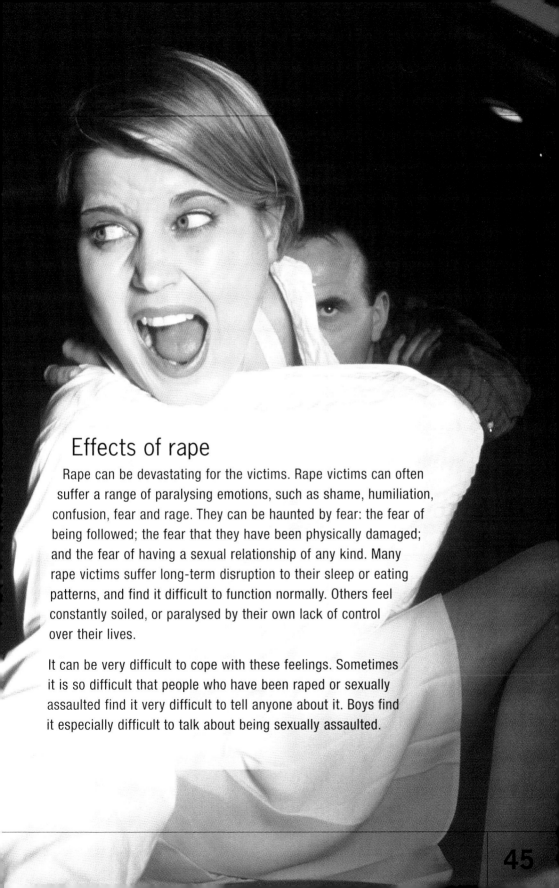

Effects of rape

Rape can be devastating for the victims. Rape victims can often
suffer a range of paralysing emotions, such as shame, humiliation,
confusion, fear and rage. They can be haunted by fear: the fear of
being followed; the fear that they have been physically damaged;
and the fear of having a sexual relationship of any kind. Many
rape victims suffer long-term disruption to their sleep or eating
patterns, and find it difficult to function normally. Others feel
constantly soiled, or paralysed by their own lack of control
over their lives.

It can be very difficult to cope with these feelings. Sometimes
it is so difficult that people who have been raped or sexually
assaulted find it very difficult to tell anyone about it. Boys find
it especially difficult to talk about being sexually assaulted.

Sex without consent

Sexual abuse

Sexual abuse includes any sexual advance carried out by an older person on a younger person (under the **age of consent**), which makes them feel uncomfortable, or which they do not like, or which hurts.

When an adult abuses a child it is always the adult's fault, never the child's.

During sexual abuse, the abuser will usually ask the victim not to tell anyone. The abuser may threaten to hurt or punish the victim if they are worried that the victim might tell. The abuser often continues to molest the other person, even if they have said they do not like it. Sometimes, an older man exposes his penis and **masturbates** himself in front of a minor, or asks the younger person to masturbate him.

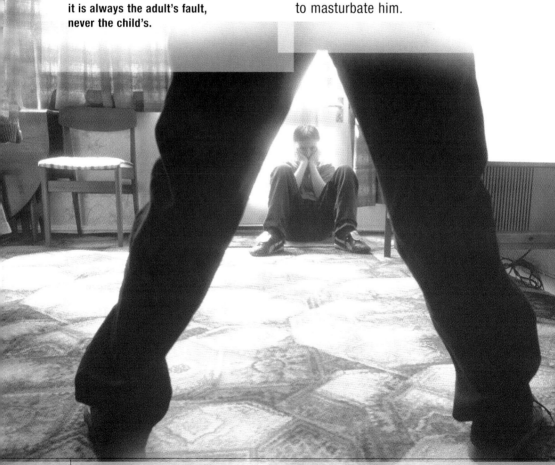

Martin's story

When Martin was twelve, the father of a friend started to abuse him. This is Martin's story:

'I just sat there. I was scared and confused and guilty. He was breathing heavily and started to masturbate himself when I didn't oblige. When it was over he drove home. On the way back he said if I ever told anyone he would say it was me. He said I would be in big trouble and my parents would not believe me. I got scared that I wasn't a proper boy. I didn't tell anyone and tried to keep away from him. But he still continued to touch me. I became withdrawn.

'When I was back on the farm, Mum and Dad saw I was quiet and they sat me down for one of their family talks. I told them. It was a great relief just to say it out loud.

'They didn't blame me at all. [They] went straight to call the local hospital, where there's a sexual assault clinic. We went in to talk to a counsellor.

'With their support and the counsellor, I was OK. I'm seventeen and I have a regular girlfriend now, and I feel good about myself. The people at the centre told me lots of boys don't tell anyone. They can end up in a bad way, not able to relate properly.

'I hope if anything like my story has happened to you or if it does in the future, you do something about it. It's much better than keeping quiet.'

Extracted from the Australian website www.secasa.com.au

Legal matters

Confidentiality

In legal terms, teenagers 'who understand the treatment' can legally receive advice from their family doctor or local birth control clinic without their parents' knowledge, even if they are under the **age of consent**. Legally, a doctor cannot break the confidentiality of the doctor/patient relationship without the patient's consent. Any teenager who is over the age of consent can legally arrange for a termination of her pregnancy, without telling her parents. If she is under-age, most doctors will try to persuade her to inform her family.

The age of consent and 'statutory rape'

Sexual intercourse with a minor (a person under the age of consent) is a serious offence – even if the minor suggested or 'consented' to having sex. In the UK, if anyone has sex with a minor under the age of thirteen, it is automatically classed as rape, known legally as 'statutory rape', and carries the same prison sentence. If anyone has **oral sex** with a minor, it is classed as sexual assault or as an act of gross indecency, and carries a lesser jail sentence.

A GP must judge whether or not a teenager understands the treatment which is being offered.

Male-female (**heterosexual**) sexual activity has a legal definition for the purposes of deciding whether 'statutory rape' has taken place. In Australia, for example, the current legal definition of 'sex' includes **oral sex** (stimulation of the genitals by the mouth) as well as slight penetration of the **vagina** by any object, including the penis.

Male-male sex (**homosexual**) usually refers to oral and **anal sex** (penetration of the anus by the penis). In some states, there is one age of consent for homosexual oral sex and a higher age for **sodomy** (anal sex between homosexuals). In some countries, homosexuality, including **lesbianism** (female-female sex) is illegal.

Age of consent

COUNTRY/state	Male-female sex	Male-male sex	Female-female sex
AUSTRALIA			
Queensland	16	16/18*	16
New South Wales	16	16/18*	16
Northern Territory	16	16/18*	No law
South Australia	16	16/17*	16
Tasmania	17	17	17
Victoria	16	16	16
Western Australia	16	16/18*	16
CANADA	14	14/18*	14
DENMARK	15	15	15
GERMANY	16	16	16
INDIA	16	Illegal	Illegal
SAUDI ARABIA	(must be married)	Illegal	Illegal
SOUTH AFRICA	16	19	19
ENGLAND, SCOTLAND AND WALES	16	16	16
N. IRELAND	17	17	17

The symbol * denotes the age of consent for **sodomy**.

People to talk to

For teenagers who are worried about a relationship or how to use **contraception** safely, for instance, it is often helpful to talk to someone they know, a parent or an adult whom they feel they can trust. It is worth remembering that adults were once young themselves and will probably have shared the same worries at some point.

If the problem needs more expert help and advice, there is a wide range of telephone contacts – many of them free of charge and most of them anonymous – where teenagers can find out more information. There are also many websites, both in the UK and Australia and around the world, which people can browse at leisure, without speaking to anyone directly. Many of the organizations listed in the information and advice section (pages 52–53) provide specialist help. They may provide a telephone service or they can suggest local agencies throughout the UK and Australia.

Accidental pregnancy

If a girl has mixed feelings about being pregnant and about the choices open to her, making a decision can be difficult and frightening. In making her choice, it may help to list those feelings and explore them. No one can be certain what all the consequences of their choice may be, but if they consider their future plans, their values and feelings, they will be able to make the best decision for them at the time. If a girl decides to keep the baby, she will not be able to hide the fact that she is pregnant for long. It is important for her to tell someone in her family that she is pregnant, as she will need their support and help during the pregnancy, and once the baby has been born.

Sexual abuse cases

If a young person is suffering sexual abuse or has been abused in the past, it can be very difficult to speak out. They may be too frightened to tell anyone, or think they will not be believed. It may take months before they pluck up the courage to seek help.

Finding someone to tell can be difficult, too. If the abuse is inside the family, the victim may want to tell a parent but feel worried that the shock may be so great that they may not be believed. There may be a school counsellor or a teacher whom the young person can trust instead. If there is no one at home or at school, they can phone a helpline, or local social services or the police.

Information and advice

The organizations and websites listed below provide a wealth of information and advice on the issues covered in this book.

Contacts in the UK

AVERT
www.avert.org
This website contains **HIV** and **AIDS** statistics, information for young people, personal stories, a history section, information on becoming infected, a young and **gay** section and free access to resources.

Brook
Unit 421, Highgate Studios, 52–79 Highgate Road, London NW5 1TL
Tel: 0800 0185 023, www.brook.org.uk
Clinics for young people up to the age of 24, for **contraception**, sexual and relationship problems.

British Pregnancy Advisory Service
Austy Manor, Wootton Wawen, Solihull, West Midlands B95 6BX
Action line: 08457 30 40 30, www.bpas.org
A national network of 40 centres offering pregnancy testing, unplanned pregnancy consultation, **abortion** and emergency contraception. Phone to make a confidential appointment with specialist staff at a centre.

Childline
Tel: 0800 1111
A free and confidential 24-hour helpline for young people with any problem.

National AIDS helpline
Tel: 0800 567 123
A free 24-hour helpline on all aspects of HIV and AIDS.

Rape Crisis Federation
7 Mansfield Road, Nottingham NG1 3FB
Tel: 0115 934 8474, www.rapecrisis.co.uk
The Rape Crisis Federation provides confidential information, advice and details of your nearest centre.

Sex Education Forum
National Children's Bureau (NCB), 8 Wakely Street, London EC1V 7QE
Tel: 020 7843 6056
Website: www.ncb.org.uk/sexed.htm
The NCB provides an email service to young people on their website. They also have information on sex and relationships for young people with a disability.

SPOD (Association to Aid the Sexual and Personal Relationships of People with a Disability)
286 Camden Road, London N7 0BJ
Tel: 020 7607 8851, Helpline: 020 7607 9191
www.spod-uk.org
SPOD provides useful information and advice on personal and sexual relationships for people with a disability.

Survivors UK
PO Box 2470, London SW9 6WQ
Tel: 020 7613 0808 (Tuesdays 7–10 p.m.)
Website: www.survivorsuk.co.uk
For boys and men who have been sexually assaulted or raped.

Terrence Higgins Trust (THT)
52–54 Gray's Inn Road, London WC1X 8JU
Tel: 0845 1221 200, www.tht.org.uk
THT is the UK's largest HIV and AIDS charity. The national helpline gives practical support, help, counselling and advice for anyone with, or concerned about, AIDS and HIV infection.

Contacts in Australia

CASA

Tel: (03) 9594 2289 (Australia-wide freecall)
The Centre Against Sexual Assault caters for adult (17 years or over) victims or survivors of sexual assault. In Australia, the local Community Policing Squad is available 24 hours a day. In Melbourne, there are two young women's refuges for 12–18 year-olds who are being physically, sexually or emotionally abused at home. There are also refuges for boys and girls.

Kids Free Confidential Helpline

Tel: 1800 551 800 (1800 Freecall numbers do not appear on phone bills)

SECASA

The South East Centre Against Sexual Assault provides a secure and confidential email service (with panic button) for kids to talk to local police at www.secasa.com.au.

NEW SOUTH WALES:
Mediguide Family Planning

North Sydney Tel: (02) 9959 5099

VICTORIA:
Women's Clinic on Richmond Hill

Richmond Tel: (03) 9427 0399

www.ninemonths.com.au

A useful guide to every aspect of having a baby in Australia.

Further reading

A Kid's First Book about Sex, by Jamie Blank; Allen & Unwin, 2001.
Australian guide to issues around sexuality for teenage girls.

Boys' Stuff, by Wayne Martino and Maria Pallotta-Chiarolli; Allen & Unwin, 2001.
Australian book on complex aspects of boys' lives, including sex, drugs, expectations and relationships.

Girls in Love, Girls Out Late and Girls Under Pressure, by Jacqueline Wilson; Doubleday, 1998.
Three novels that deal with teenage dating.

4 Girls: a below-the-bra-guide to the female body and *4 Boys: a below-the-belt guide to the male body*; Family Planning Association, 1999.
Booklets for 13–17 year-olds giving factual information about sex and puberty.

Hair in Funny Places, by Babette Cole; Red Fox, 2001.
Humorous UK illustrated book about puberty, for girls.

Glossary

abortion
ending a pregnancy by surgery or drugs, usually in the early stages before twelve weeks (also called a termination)

abstinence
choosing not to have any form of sexual intercourse until a steady relationship or marriage

age of consent
the legal age at which one person can have sexual intercourse with another, of their own free will

AIDS
The shortened form of Acquired Immune Deficiency Syndrome, which is the name often given to the later stages of HIV infection

anal sex
penetration of the anus by a penis

bisexual
a person who is sexually attracted to men and women

cervical, cervix
concerning the closed opening to the womb, which is found at the top of the vagina

chlamydia
a sexually transmitted infection that, if left untreated, can cause infertility in women

clitoris
the small, highly sensitive bump under the hood of the labia majora, at the top of the vulva. The clitoris is the origin of the female orgasm.

condom (female)
a latex device worn inside the vagina to prevent pregnancy and infection

condom (male)
a latex sheath worn over the penis to prevent pregnancy and infection

contraception, contraceptive
a device or pill that prevents pregnancy by stopping male sperm from fertilizing the female egg

cystitis
a urinary infection that causes pain when urinating

ejaculate, ejaculation
milky white semen that has spurted out of the penis tip

erect, erection
stiffening and enlargement of the penis when sexually excited

foreskin
the sleeve of skin that covers the head of the penis

gay
a person who sexually desires someone of the same sex

Genito-urinary medicine (GUM) clinic
a clinic where STIs are diagnosed and treated in confidence

gonorrhoea
a sexually transmitted disease that can be effectively treated when diagnosed

hepatitis B
a virus transmitted in infected blood, causing fever and jaundice

herpes
an incurable viral disease causing outbreaks of blisters on the skin

heterosexual
men and women who sexually desire the opposite sex

HIV

the shortened form of Human Immunodeficiency Virus. HIV attacks and destroys the body's immune system.

homosexuals

men who sexually desire other men

lesbians, lesbianism

women who sexually desire other women

masturbation

giving sexual pleasure to one's own body in order to reach a state of orgasm

monogamy

choosing to have sex with only one partner

oral sex

giving sexual pleasure to a partner by mouth in order to help them reach a state of orgasm

orgasm (female)

sensations of pleasure in the clitoris leading to involuntary muscle contractions in the vagina

orgasm (male)

involuntary muscle contractions at the base of the penis, giving sexual pleasure and leading to ejaculation

ovulation

the time when a female egg descends into the womb from the fallopian tube and is ready to be fertilized

rhythm method

avoiding sexual intercourse around the time of ovulation

scrotum

the loose pouch of skin that holds the testicles

semen

the milky-white ejaculate containing sperm, also commonly called 'spunk' or 'come'

sexual intercourse

penetration and stimulation of the vagina or anus by a penis, often resulting in an orgasm

smear test

a medical test used to detect pre-cancerous cells in the cervix. A smear test is usually carried out by a nurse and should be done once a woman becomes sexually active.

sodomy

anal sex between homosexuals

spermicide

a gel or substance, usually contained within barrier contraceptives, that kills sperm and prevents it from reaching the female egg

STI

a sexually transmitted infection

syphilis

a sexually transmitted infection that can be treated effectively when diagnosed

testicles

a pair of male organs that produce sperm. Testicles are located in the scrotum.

unfertilized eggs

female eggs that have not met with male sperm and so will not go on to develop into a baby

unprotected sex

sexual intercourse without using contraception, particularly condoms

vagina

an internal tube that opens in the vulva and ends in the cervix

virgin, virginity

the state of not having had sex

vulva

the female genital area comprising the inner and outer labia and the opening of the vagina and urethra

Index

Titles in the *Need to Know* series include:

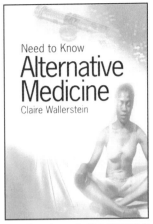

Hardback   0 431 09808 5

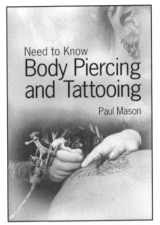

Hardback   0 431 09818 2

Hardback   0 431 09809 3

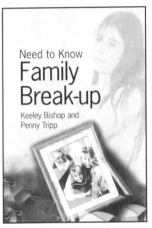

Hardback   0 431 09810 7

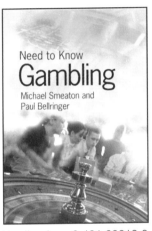

Hardback   0 431 09819 0

Hardback   0 431 09811 5

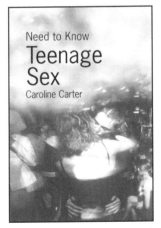

Hardback   0 431 09821 2

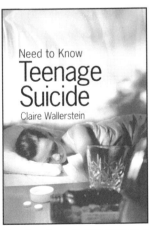

Hardback   0 431 09820 4

Find out about the other titles in this series on our website www.heinemann.co.uk/library